DINOSAUR LIVES

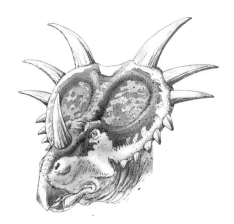

written by Priscilla Hannaford
illustrated by S Boni *and* L R Galante

Ladybird

Contents

What Were the Dinosaurs?

Millions of years ago, long before there were people, dinosaurs lived on Earth. The dinosaurs were **reptiles**, like crocodiles or lizards. The word 'dinosaur' means 'terrible lizard' in Greek.

Some dinosaurs *were* terrible. They had strong teeth and claws and were fierce fighters. But not all dinosaurs were like that. Many were peaceful and ate only plants.

The biggest dinosaurs were 50 metres long. The smallest were only the size of chickens.

When Did They Live?

Dinosaurs first appeared about 220 **million** years ago. They lived on Earth for about 155 million years – far longer than people have been here.

| **Number of years ago** | 4,600 million Earth formed | 3,800 million First living things |

190 million
First mammals

220 million
First dinosaurs

145 million
First birds

65 million
Dinosaurs die out

Not all the different types of dinosaurs lived at the same time. As one group of dinosaurs died out, another group **evolved** to take its place.

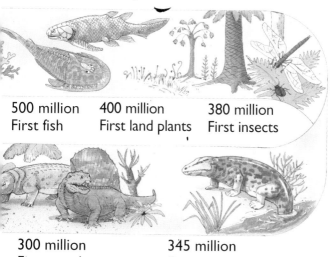

500 million
First fish

400 million
First land plants

380 million
First insects

300 million
First reptiles

345 million
First amphibians

55 million
Age of mammals

2 million
First humans

Present
day

How We Know

Clues about what dinosaurs were like
are hidden in the ground. The bones
of dinosaurs became trapped in the
layers of mud and sand and turned to
rock, forming **fossils**. **Scientists** learn
about dinosaurs by studying the fossils.

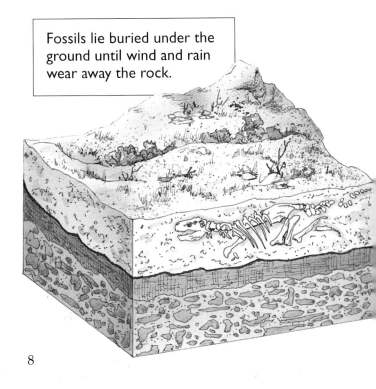

Fossils lie buried under the
ground until wind and rain
wear away the rock.

Sometimes whole **skeletons** are found. This one belongs to one of the giant plant eaters.

Camarasaurus skeleton

Scientists need to work very carefully to remove the fossils as they can break very easily.

Fierce Meat Eaters

Some dinosaurs hunted and ate meat.
They had long jaws and sharp teeth.
They ran on their two back legs and
had long, heavy tails. They used their
front **limbs**, which were very short, to
help to catch and hold animals.

Carnotaurus lived in South
America. It had two horns,
like a bull.

Carnotaurus

Compsognathus

Dromiceiomimus

Compsognathus was the smallest of all the dinosaurs. It was only the size of a chicken.

Dromiceiomimus looked a bit like an ostrich. It could run very fast.

Tyrannosaurus

Tyrannosaurus was the biggest meat eating dinosaur. It grew to twelve metres long.

Gentle Giants

The largest dinosaurs did not eat meat,
only plants. They had huge bodies and
very long necks. They were so heavy
they had to walk on all four legs. They
had to spend most of their time eating.

Amargasaurus

Amargasaurus had spikes
and frills down its neck
and back. It lived in
South America.

Diplodocus used its long neck to reach leaves at the tops of trees. Sometimes it would stand on its **hind** legs to reach even higher.

Diplodocus

Other Plant Eaters

Other, smaller plant eaters could walk on their hind legs, like the meat eaters. They were about as tall as the meat eaters, but had much bigger bodies. Their teeth were specially **adapted** for eating and chewing plants.

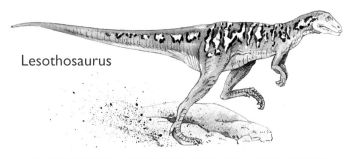

Lesothosaurus

Dinosaurs like *Lesothosaurus* could eat all sorts of plants, even prickly pine needles.

Iguanodon was one
of the first dinosaurs
to be discovered.

Iguanodon

The two footed plant eaters had special **pouches**
in their cheeks, where they held food while it
was being chewed.

Plated Dinosaurs

Other groups of dinosaurs evolved from the two footed plant eaters. One of these groups had plates and spines sticking up along their backs.

Scientists think the plates may have been used as armour, or to collect heat from the sun to help to keep the dinosaur warm.

Yingshanosaurus had huge spines on its shoulders. It lived in China.

Yingshanosaurus

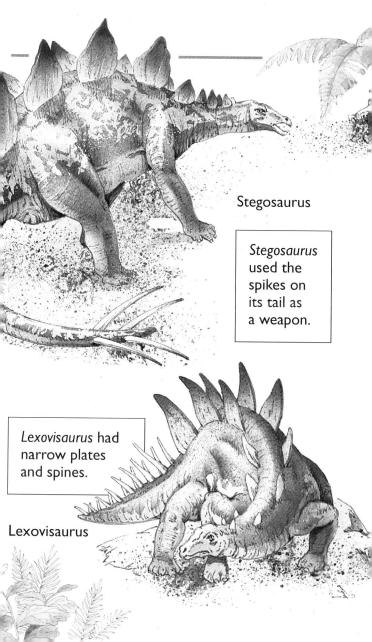

Stegosaurus

Stegosaurus used the spikes on its tail as a weapon.

Lexovisaurus had narrow plates and spines.

Lexovisaurus

Armoured Dinosaurs

The **armoured** dinosaurs were plant
eaters. They had heavy, bony plates
all over their backs. They needed
plenty of armour to defend themselves
against the larger meat eaters.

This armour was so heavy that they
had to walk on all fours.

Euoplocephalus's head was covered
with armoured plates – even its
eyelids had special plates!

Euoplocephalus

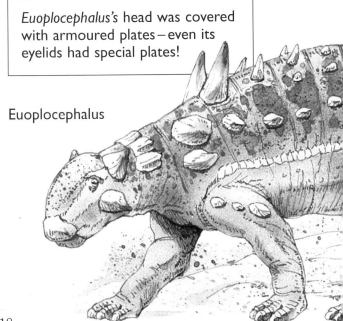

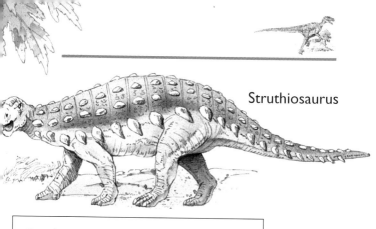

Struthiosaurus

Struthiosaurus was about the size of a sheep. It lived in central Europe.

Some armoured dinosaurs had clubs on the end of their tails.

Horned Dinosaurs

The last dinosaur group to evolve was that of the horned dinosaurs. They had huge armoured **frills** round their necks and horns on their faces. The frills and horns made their heads very heavy so they walked on all four legs.

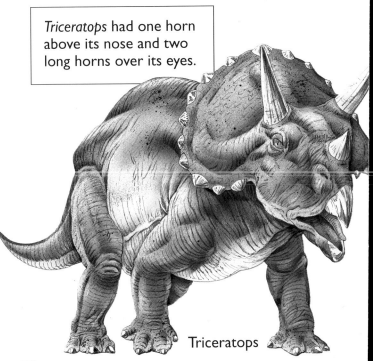

Triceratops had one horn above its nose and two long horns over its eyes.

Triceratops

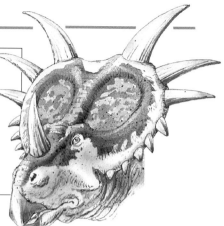

The horns helped to defend these dinosaurs against the meat eaters. *Styracosaurus* also had spikes on its neck frill.

Styracosaurus

Most horned dinosaurs were about the size of a present-day rhinoceros. Their bodies looked like a rhino's body, but their heads were very different.

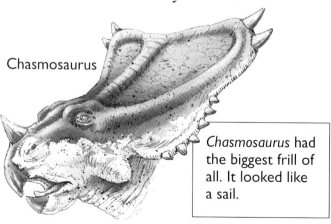

Chasmosaurus

Chasmosaurus had the biggest frill of all. It looked like a sail.

21

Dinosaurs Laid Eggs

Dinosaurs laid eggs, but few nests
have been found. This may be because
they laid their eggs on top of cliffs or
in holes in the ground. Scientists
however have found nests belonging
to *Maiasaura*, a two footed plant eater.

Maiasauras laid their eggs
in huge nests. Several nests
have been found near to
one another.

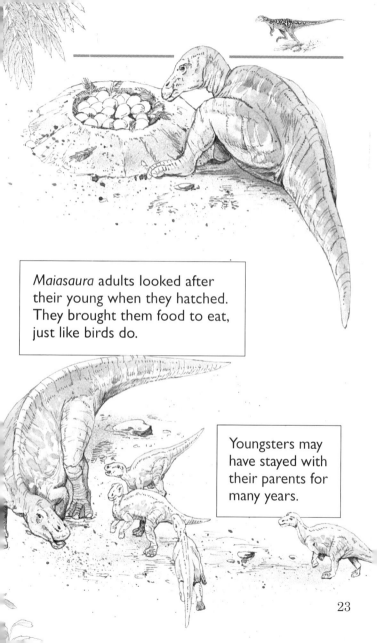

Maiasaura adults looked after
their young when they hatched.
They brought them food to eat,
just like birds do.

Youngsters may
have stayed with
their parents for
many years.

23

In the Sea

Plesiosaur

While dinosaurs lived on the ground, other reptiles lived in the sea. They all breathed air and came to the water's surface to breathe.

Pliosaurs were fast swimmers. They swam by flapping their large fins up and down.

Pliosaur

Icthyosaurs ate fish and flying reptiles that lived close to the sea.

Icthyosaur

In the Sky

Dinosaurs couldn't fly, but there were other animals around at the time that could. They were called pterosaurs. They looked more like bats than birds.

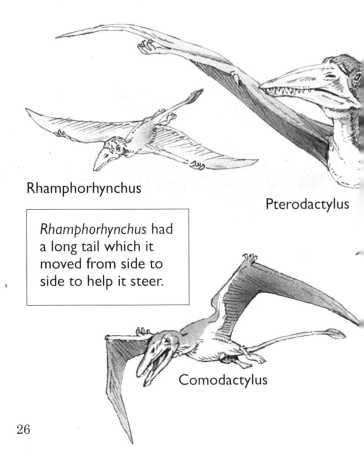

Rhamphorhynchus

Pterodactylus

Rhamphorhynchus had a long tail which it moved from side to side to help it steer.

Comodactylus

Their wings were made of leathery skin stretched between their arms and back legs. All the pterosaurs had large heads with jaws of teeth or horny beaks.

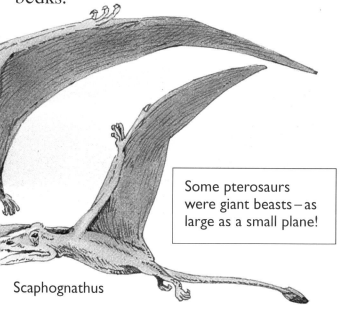

Some pterosaurs were giant beasts – as large as a small plane!

Scaphognathus

Scientists can tell what a pterosaur ate by studying its jaws. *Scaphognathus* ate fish.

After the Dinosaurs

The dinosaurs and the swimming and flying reptiles died out about 65 million years ago. We do not know why. In their place **mammals** began to take over the world.

The Earth's large forests also died away and **grasslands** began to appear.

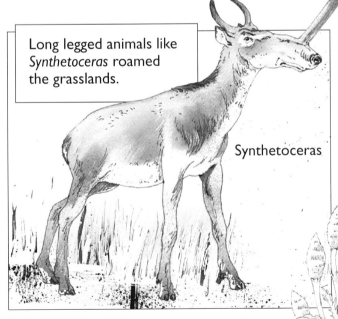

Long legged animals like *Synthetoceras* roamed the grasslands.

Synthetoceras

Amebelodon

Amebelodon
is an
ancestor
of the elephant.

Protocetus

Some mammals
moved to live
in the seas.
They evolved
into whales.

Icaronycteris

Pterosaurs were
replaced by bats,
like this one.

Glossary

Adapt To change over a period of time for a special reason.

Ancestor An animal in the past that has a very similar body shape to a present-day animal.

Armoured Covered with a hard outer layer.

Evolve To change gradually over hundreds of years.

Fossil The remains of a plant or animal from millions of years ago, preserved in stone.

Frill A stiff piece of bone round a dinosaur's neck or along its back.

Grassland A large area of land covered in grass with very few trees.

Hind The back legs of an animal.

Limb An animal's leg and, sometimes, arm.

Mammal An animal that gives birth to live young and feeds them on milk.

Million One thousand thousand.

Pouch A baggy area of skin.

Reptile A cold-blooded animal with a scaly skin. Most reptiles lay eggs.

Scientist A person who studies facts about the world we live in.

Skeleton The bones of an animal arranged in the correct position of the body.